EXALTATIONS

EXALTATIONS

Songs of the Soul

Volume III

Camille Hamilton Adams Helminski

Cover: Design by Matthew Helminski; original photo by Camille Helminski

First edition published 2025
by Sweet Lady Press,
an imprint of Threshold Books

© Camille Hamilton Adams Helminski, 2025

Paperback ISBN: 978-0-939660-63-6
E-book ISBN: 978-0-939660-64-3

Typesetting by Daniel Thomas Dyer

Rose illustration and Rose logo by Cara Helminski Chadwick
Iris ornament: drawing by Camille Helminski

All rights reserved. No part of this publication may be reproduced or utilized in any form or by any means, electronic or mechanical, including photocopying, or by any information storage and retrieval system, without prior written permission from Sweet Lady Press.

Library of Congress Control Number: 2025944610

SWEET LADY PRESS
London, Istanbul, Escondido
sweetladypress.com

*In the Name of God, the Infinitely Compassionate,
the Continually Merciful.
Say, "Hu is God, Hu is One (Unified Reality)—
'Allah', Hu, the Eternal Source Without Need
(Satisfier of All Needs).*

[Qur'an, Surah al-Ihklas, 112:1–2]

*Truly, Divine Reality—Hu is the Most Exalted, Most Great
[Allaha—Huwa al-'Aliyy al-Kabir].
Don't you see that God sends down rain from the sky,
which the earth drinks and then becomes green?
Truly, Allah is the Infinitely Subtle, All-Aware
[Allaha al-Latifun Khabir].
To Him/Her belongs all that is in the heavens
and upon the earth.
And indeed, God is the Truly Rich Without Need
(the Source from which all emanates),
the One Worthy of Praise.
[Wa inna Allaha Huwa Ghaniyy al-Hamid.]*

[Qur'an, Surah al-Hajj, 22:62–64]

Table of Contents

Preface
ix

1. A Song in Praise of the Sacred 1
2. A Breath of Love 4
3. Ah! This Beauty!! 6
4. In the Palace of Your Love 8
5. In the Name of All 9
6. A Mouth to Drink Your Love 12
7. The State of Greenness 13
8. "Am I not Your Lord?" 17
9. O Beloved! 19
10. Freedom Celebrations 20
11. The Rain is Pouring Love 21
12. *Adab için* 22
13. Bismillah arRahman arRahim 23
14. In the Morning 24
15. Your Joy is our joy! 25
16. Planting Joy 28
17. Exaltations 30
18. The Call of Love 31
19. The Day is Promised 33
20. So Many Mornings 35
21. Bow in Worship! 37
22. The Breath of Life 38
23. The DNA of Joy 40
24. Signs of Life 42
25. Roses of Your Love 44
26. Don't You Love the Rain! 45
27. Sparkles on the Sea 46

28. Full Moon 47
29. At the Table of Your Grace 49
30. Remembrances of Love 51
31. Giving Birth 52
32. On the Street of Your Love 54
33. Moment by Moment 56
34. Moments of Grace 57
35. *Hasbiyallah!* 58
36. *Ulul Albab* 60
37. Songs of Praise 61
38. Living in the Miraculous 62
39. A Moment's Breath! 65
40. From Darkness into Light! 66
41. Gracious Rains 67
42. *Subhanallah!* 68
43. Exaltations of Your Love 69
44. Your Light Keeps Pouring! 70
45. Disappearing Within Your Love 72
46. Witness to Your Love 74
47. The Garden of Your Exaltations 76
48. Morning Opens 78
49. Bees of Your Haven 80
50. Eternal Love 82

Reflection Notes
87

Preface

Bismillah arRahman arRahim

Becoming Nur

You are always with us.[i]
We seek and seek
until
You find us,
and we know
You have never left,
but are always right here, beside us,
within us,
looking when we look,
listening when we listen,
speaking when we call Your Name,
and answering us by Heart . . .

We begin in the name of God and glorify that one who enlivens us, guides us, restores, and returns us to Herself/ Himself. Many ways have been gifted to us to perceive,

---

[i] See Qur'an, *Surah al Hadid* 57:4:
He is with you wherever you are.
See also *Surah Taha* 20:46, when the Divine intimated to Moses and Aaron as they were facing Pharaoh:
Hu *said, "Do not be fearful.* [La takhafaa.] *Truly, I am with you both.* [Innanee ma'akuma.] *I hear and I see.* [Asma'u wa araa.]*"*

to witness that Presence within us, through us, among us, encompassing us, blessing us with Grace. We offer this gathering of moments, as a witnessing of that Continual Blessing Pouring. May we each open to radiate that Light of Love further throughout this magnificent Creation, as we more and more fully witness the Garden that is all around us (*Dem bu dem bu dem*).[ii] May we each become "that niche in which is a candle shining with a radiance brighter than the dawn."[iii] *Nur ala Nur ala Nur Olsun* (May it be Light upon Light upon Light)!

For many years now we have listened at the feet of beloved Mevlana Jalaluddin Rumi and Hazrati Shams of Tabriz who have opened for us a deepening with the meanings of the Qur'an, and the Way of beloved Prophet Muhammad, and all the prophets and lovers of God, for which we are eternally grateful.

When we call upon the Beloved, that One who is All-Hearing, All-Seeing, most surely in the very best moment, that Infinitely Gracious One responds. As Mevlana Rumi reminds us through his *Mathnawi*:

> Without need, the Almighty God
> doesn't give anything to anyone.

[ii] "Moment, this Moment, this moment!"
[iii] Mevlana Jalaluddin Rumi, *Mathnawi*, Book I: Prologue, referencing Qur'an, *Surah an-Nur* 24:35:
> *God is the Light of the heavens and the earth.*
> *The parable of His light is,*
> *as it were, that of a niche containing a lamp;*
> *the lamp is enclosed in glass, the glass like a radiant star;*
> *lit from a blessed tree—an olive-tree*
> *that is neither of the east nor of the west—*
> *the oil of which would almost give light*
> *even though fire had not touched it: light upon light!*
> *God guides to His light the one who wills to be guided;*
> *and God offers parables to human beings,*
> *since God has full knowledge of all things.*

If the earth had not been needed by the world,
the Sustainer of all beings
would not have created it;
and if this quaking earth
had not needed mountains,
He would not have formed such sublime heights;
and if there had not been need
of the heavenly spheres,
from non-existence He would not have opened
   the Seven Skies.
The sun and moon and these stars—
how did they come forth except through need?
Need, then, is the net for all things that exist:
the human being has means
in proportion to his or her need.
So, quickly, increase your need, O needy one,
that the Sea of Abundance
may surge up in Lovingkindness.

*

An endarkened mole, once purified,
grows wings,
becomes a bird,
and flies,
glorifying its Creator;
every moment, in the Rose-garden
of thanksgiving to God,
it will yield a hundred sweet notes,
like the nightingale.

*

The word is like the nest,
and meaning is the bird:
the body is the riverbed,
and spirit is the rolling water.

*

The seed-husks floating on the water
come from the fruits of the Invisible Garden;
seek the kernels (the seeds of Love) of those husks
within that Garden.[iv]

As beloved Rabi'a al-'Adawiyye has said, "I sent my heart to this world, so that it might see this world. Then I told it, 'Go to the world of meaning, and see the meaning, too.' It didn't return to me."[v]

May we immerse ourselves in the Enlightening, Restorative Meanings of Our Beloved Sustainer, and *be* together in that Exalted Garden, radiating Light further into this world. *Alhamdulillah! Subhanallah! Ya Rabb al-'Alameen!*
Ya Nur!
Ya Haqq!
Ya Wadud!
Huuuuuuu

~ Camille
'Eid al-Adha, 2025, Escondido, "the Hidden realm"

[iv] Mevlana Jalaluddin Rumi, *Mathnawi* II: 3274–80; 3287–88; 3293; 3297–98.

[v] *Rumi's Sun: the Teachings of Shams of Tabriz*, translated by Refik Algan and Camille Helminski, p.280.

A Song in Praise of the Sacred

Bismillah arRahman arRahim
A new morning,
a night of sleep—
such graces—
to be renewed,
resurrected
into the soft ocean
of Your Presence
holding
our possibilities.
Guide this hand
to pluck the strings
of the harp of deeds
to sound the best notes,
in harmony,
with generosity,
mindful of all,
who must hear and feel,
connected through this air
in vibrancy.
O my Lord,
how can we ever express
Your Blessing,
when You express us,
instilled
with Your Breath—
it is but You

singing songs
of Yourself
through every heart
You have ever created,
of which we yet
understand so little—
how Your miracles
are wrought!
Entwined,
intricately woven,
every system
perfect
in its co-functioning
to make us move,
in Your Love,
from here to Eternity
and back in a flash—
through doorways
and windows
that keep opening
everywhere.
These doorways
and windows
of remembrance
structured
into our very DNA—
we've been gifted
infinite avenues
of knowing You,
of exploring
our capacities
for Praise
of Your intimate Beauty,
Your infinite Power.

Your surf,
upon these rocky shores,
that rises with Your sun
rains
upon the fiery slopes
and causes tendrilled ferns
to flourish,
gaining footholds,
spreading Your greenness
and Your incumbent fruitfulness
even from amidst
molten glass!
You are Hope,
You are Resilience;
You are Renewal;
You are our breath,
our moments,
our love,
now and eternally,
Ya Wadud!

A Breath of Love

I love
to love
You,
my Lord,
my Breath,
my very soul—
how is it
I can even find
words to speak
from within
this velvet darkness
where all awaits
Creation—
You choose
some strand
to be knit
together
of sounds
awakening
into the Light
of the dawn.
Moisture on the air,
in the air,
through the air,
arrives
resounding
with

Your Purpose.

Dolphins
arc
in the sunrise,

while
Your Ocean
spreads out
vast
and still,
and a single
bird
song
lilts—
a Messenger
from Your Heart
to this
drop
of the Ocean
of Your Love,
Ya Rabb al-'Alameen!
O Gracious Bestower
of Life!
Ya Sami, Ya Basir,
Ya Wasi!
Ya Nur, Ya Wadud!

Ah! This Beauty!!

This Beauty!
Ah! This Beauty!!
How do You
find Yourself?
Unearthing
our doubt
and disrepair,
the spring
of Your Love
washes clear
our debris—
the sticks and stones
of old moments,
no longer
vibrant for us,
needing
to be moved
for the water
of Life
to reach
our fields,
laid out
in the glory
of Your Sun.
From the mountains,
we flow
with You,

pure oxygen
and hydrogen
doubled,
clasped
in Your Love.
Your magnetism
pulls us
to the Sea
where we sing
songs
of the heights
and the depths
of Your Loving,
forever pouring
through
every breath
of air and sky
and sea and earth
pulsing with subtle Spirit
sparkling,
dancing,
everywhere.

In the Palace of Your Love

O *Allah!*
In the Palace of Your Love
there are also challenges.
Can we rest with You,
even so,
You seem to want to know.
Duress can make diamonds—
if we are alive
with Your Knowing:
Love is not empty of pain;
birth is a journey
through constriction
into Light.

And always You are with us.
How can we not call out Your Name?
O *Allah,*
Ya Quddus!
Ya Wadud!
Ya Karim!

In the Name of All

Mary,
gentleness expounding,
waves of Mercy
upon the shore
of our being.

Who are we?

Who are you?
Spirit breathing,
being breathed.

A son arrived,
to you—a daughter—
Breath to breath,
hand to hand,
we hold each other—

the banks of a stream
leading
to the ocean,
sea to shining Sea.

Diamonds explode
in the Sun
of these hearts,

these minds
that would unearth
the songs
of Your Love.

Mine shafts
let in the light—
pierced
to the center.

Molten magma
bubbles up
and forms new promontories,
treasures for ferns
to kiss
in the bright morning.

Precious, virgin soil,
awaiting
Your creation,
with the spray of the sea
and the song of the birds
already harvesting
nearby hills,
mountains of Your Making.

Up and down,
In and out,
You weave
Your tapestry
of Glory,
studded with gems
and tied

to the tent pegs
of Your Power
uniting
Heaven and Earth,
Inner and Outer.

*Peace,
a Word*
from the Most Magnificent,
the Most Generous,
the Most Compassionate,
our Sustainer,
Most Merciful.

*Salamun
qawlan
min Rabbin
Rahim.*

*Subhanallah!
Ya Rabb al-'Alameen,*
of Paradise
and its fountains,
the Creator.
*Ya Khaliq, Ya Bari, Ya Mussawir,
Ya Awwal, Ya Akhir, Ya Warith.*

A Mouth to Drink Your Love

Every particle of our being
is a mouth to drink Your Love.
Through that Love
even the bitter becomes sweet.
What is sweetness in Reality
but a taste that resonates
within the heart as Love—
we recognize You with every breath we take,
for it is You who are the Giver,
our Mother, our Father,
our Source—
cherishing us in every moment,
from before the beginning
and long after our return,
purifying our hearts
that we might be able to hear
Your Word.
O You who are
The First, The Last,
Infinitely Compassionate,
Most Holy Pure,
O Infinitely Loving One!
Ya Awwal, Ya Ahkir,
Ya Rahman, Ya Quddus,
Ya Wadud!

The State of Greenness

So many gifts—
an eagle soaring
catching the wind
of Your Grace,
a fawn mewing,
tiny, lost behind the barn,
found, as we return,
gracing the field
with its mother's care
as they crossed
the Sea of grass.
Bird songs
that thrill the heart
as trills traverse the scales,
in a delicate language
we have yet to learn,
but feel.
Hummingbird dances—
through azalea heaven,
so rosy, even in the rain.
Lilac fragrance—
heavy on the breeze
surrounding this house
and gracing its table
where so many have sat,
over unfolding years,
to partake

of the nourishment
You provide.
Thank You, for granting
the capacity
to make quiche,
and cherry pie,
to feed these dear hearts,
this new family
sustained
by Your Breath—
which they readily extend
to all who come
within the realms
of their ken.
Neighbors help
each other
here,
amid the hills
of greenness,
and welcome strangers
from parts unknown
of Your Vast Creation.
Children rise amid the grass,
the veggies and the flowers,
venturing along the streams,
and trails of blueberries,
and moss and fern.

Spring beauties
still grace
the souls of trees
nearby,
and ancient stones

speak
of long-ago
passers-by
who settled awhile
to regard the sun
and count
its days of passing
and the stars
that brightly beam
across the Milky Way's
traversal!

Even Northern Lights
sometimes dance
here
on summer evenings,
and fairy spirits
in the grass,
and blossoms
hanging heavy,
on the shrubs
of Rhododendron
Viburnum and Beauty.

Water springs
from out the earth
in such delicious
freshness,
no where on earth
is there a sweeter taste
of water, unsullied
by human creation.
Pouring forth,

it washes our bones,
our teeth,
and clears the toxins
from this frame
that would house
Your Love,
moved by Spirit
to sing the praises
of all Your Gifts—
with deepest gratitude—
that find us here,
partaking now,
and always,
at Your Eternal Table.

"Am I not Your Lord?"

A fretless instrument—
why worry
about "ownership"?
Don't we know
to Whom we belong?

Markings on wood
can correspond
to angelic voices,
symphonies
sung in heaven—

what wonders abound!

Tapping time,
we dance
in figure-eights—
eternally circling
here
and back again—
seeking Your Face;

yet You
are right before us,
beside us,
in our very breath—

oh, yes!
"Yes,"
and again, "Yes!"

O Beloved!

O Beloved,
Beloved,
while awaiting return
You grace me with solace—
the birds,
the trees,
the leaves,
the breeze
alive with Your fragrance.

Freedom Celebrations

Just at the turning
of the day
to night
Your jubilation
flashes
in the dimming light—
fire flies!
On wings
of such delicacy,
pilots would be jealous
of Your celebrations,
if they stopped
to think
how on earth
it is done.

The Rain is Pouring Love

The rain
is pouring Love
and I drink it,
readily,
from my vista
of the trees—
Greenness
keeps on coming,
bursting, from the Unseen.
I blink,
and another leaf
extends
into habitable space
for birds to rest
and squirrels
to scramble
as they seek
their nourishment.
Continually providing,
You fill our plates,
even in the midst of winter,
fruit comes to our *mihrab*,
and like Mary,
we wonder
at Your Grace:
"See how God provides!"

Adab için

Call and response
of frogs,
outside our window.
They know,
shouldn't we?—
how to remember,
and assemble
in another world
of Sound.
Small creatures,
loud voices;
sometimes the smallest
can awaken
us all,
crying out
in this wilderness
to come,
be, in Love.

Bismillah arRahman arRahim

O *Allah!*
Awaiting Your Word,
everyday new leaves unfurl
amazed
by Your Beauty!

In the Morning

Bismillah arRahman arRahim!
Thank you!
For a moment's respite,
a hummingbird's nest,
quail voices in the morning.
You are
as You praise Yourself!
Beauty abounds
and waters keep flowing.

Your Joy is our joy!

So many doves,
and multitudes of sparrows,
but only one hawk—
it waits upon Your tower.
What does it see
from its vantage point,
lofty in Your sky?
A city of lovers?
Human beings out to seek
their daily bread?
Cars congested on Your highways,
as we are all drawn
to some work
to feed our families
and ourselves?
What if we were to turn
and make that seeking silent
inward
to find You,
who are the Source
of all the food that flows,
first through the invisible,
before it can be seen.
What if we were to journey
there, to the threshold
of Your Palace,
whose doors open

to the Infinity of Your Loving
that pours the grace
of every day that rises in our minds?
Your Joy is our joy.
Our sadness is our own,
when we forget
that *You are always with us.*
We seek and seek
until
You find us,
and we know
You have never left,
but are always right here, beside us,
within us,
looking when we look,
listening when we listen,
speaking when we call Your Name,
and answering us by Heart,
when Love flows through every pore,
as we turn to pour Your grace,
filling another's cup,
of someone who is longing
and has not yet found
a way
to open that inner door,
but soon will know
that, yes,
You love to love
through each of us,
each human being,
each plant, each leaf,
each animal, each bird,
through whom You teach us
of the miracles of grace,

of gratitude,
of strength,
as Your Brilliance
more and more is seen—
so bright that we must stop,
and simply bask in its Radiance,
and be renewed,
enlivened
with Your Love.

Planting Joy:

Morning Meditations 1

Bismillah ar-Rahman ar-Rahim

A new day,
and the moss rose
has rooted.
All praise be to You
who Open
the floodgates of being—
that a piece of root
dug from soil in the North
might be transplanted
and stretch out root-fibers
in new earth,
to receive its nourishment,
translating leaves to surge
into the fresh spring air.
We, too, find our places
drawn by heart
and circumstance
and reconnect nerve networks
among friends
and new acquaintances.
Birds fly far,
and butterflies,
yet know intrinsically
when they are home,

hatching new families
of winged creatures
with the breath of dawn.

Ya Fatah, al-'Azim!
Ya Wadud, al-'Alim!
Ya 'Aziz, al-Karim!

What miracles
You open
every moment,
every day,
in our hair and skin,
in our voices,
in our ears,
in the tuning of our hearts
to the Song
underlying all vibration—
You can be seen;
You can be known.
Subhanallah!
Ya Rabb
al-'Alameen.
You are here with us,
in every pulse
of our being;
we are not alone.

Exaltations

Your sun has risen,
and the birds gather
to sit in its glow.
Rosy to the east
and Rosy to the west,
how does the sky know?
You whisper Your Presence
in the softest voice,
only awakening those
who were deeply
listening,
watching,
for Your arrival.
A whole flock of birds
has gathered on the branches
of the cell tower, flying
in from all directions.
May we be of the people
who gather in remembrance,
receptive,
singing Your Name.
Glory, glory be to You,
O Almighty God,
Ya Hu, al-'Azim!

The Call of Love

Bismillah
ar-Rahman
ar-Rahim!
How wondrous
is Your Music
that flows
from the Unseen
through our hearts
to instruments
of wood and steel
or string
of the internal
makings of a cat,
or the hair
of a horse's tail,
or petroleum
reformulated
into plastic
molded
by extrusion
even as
the molten lava
takes shape
upon this earth
and ore
is mined
from out the layers

of millennium.

A gourd,
a rattle,
a turtle shell,
drums of skin,
there is music
everywhere,
resounding
for these ears
and hearts
that You have made.

And the birds,
such tiny beings,
whose voices
reach
through the skies
from neighborhood
to neighborhood
transcending fences;

Your Messengers
vibrate everywhere
with the call
of Love.

The Day is Promised

The Day is promised.
It does not say
anyone
will be left
in darkness.
For we will see—
we will witness
You,
the Giver of Gifts
that pour over
all our stoniness,
dissolving us
into the Light
of Your Grace,
so how could
our hearts swerve
from the Truth
of that Glance—
Your Eye
that holds us
Fast
in Your Seeing,
so that we
cannot turn away
from such Beauty
to remember
any other thing

but Your Love,
and stand
in open acquiescence
to Your Will
that has become us,
becoming,
quite suitable
to each and every one
of us,
for we were made
in the Most Beautiful
proportions
and fit
perfectly
within the dimensions
of Your Grace—
You have
sized us
up into the heavens
of Your Longing
and opened us wide
into the fields of Your Being
and planted us
firmly
in the ground of Your Knowing
so how could we forget,
ever,
Your Love?
Ya Wadud,
Ya Wadud,
Ya Wadud!

So Many Mornings

So many mornings
open
with Your Presence—
how could we see
without Your eyes?

So many nights
blossom
with Your whispers—
how could we hear
without Your ears?

Night and day
You grow in us,
through us,
around us,
beyond "us."

What is there to say
but "You love us,
and we love You!"

And when the moment
of return arrives,
You

are all
there Is!

Bow in Worship!

Stillness . . .
"Be still
and know
that I am God."
"Bow
in worship
and draw near."
Put the pencil down,
be empty
of any thing,
or place,
but here,
held
in Your Embrace.

The Breath of Life

Your stars still shine
in the western sky,
even though the dawn
approaches.
Coffee—
what a blessing;
it makes me smile
to think how many centuries
friends
have been drinking
this brown potion.
Bitter and yet sweet—
it makes our hearts leap,
for You awaken our senses;
You open our hearts.
Dervishes do dishes
in the *tekke*.
They grind coffee,
and shop
in Your market.
They serve
this golden-brown liquid
in little cups,
and gather
late into the night
to speak
of all the multitude of blessings

that keep pouring
at our feet.
How could we deny
all the grace that comes,
flying in from outer lands,
hearts that visit,
hand to hand,
and dance and whirl.
Songs of mystic lovers
pour from our lips
as, moment by moment,
You kiss us
with the Breath
of Life.
Ya Hayy,
Ya Hayy!
Ya Qayyum!

The DNA of Joy

Sweet rememberings . . .
"Plant what brings you
joy":
let us
let the seedlings
surge
into the air
of Your Love,
and nurture
them with the rain
of thanksgiving
and the sun
of remembrance,
the iron of fortitude
and the selenium
of forbearance,
conducting
our surging symphony
of resonance
with You.
DNA twins
keep reproducing
by their own mirroring,
and manifold
abundance
flies,
like dandy

lion seeds
on the wind,
finding their way
into fertile hearts,
where new
plants
of greening joy
arise—
singing
songs of Praise
for
You—
as spinning star globes
dance and shine,
in the brightness—
the Light of Your Love,
Ya Nur ala Nur ala Nur!

Signs of Life

I marvel at your strength!
How you stay upright,
through years of wind and storms!
Slender trunk rising,
yet a full-blown crown of feathered fronds—
nurtured by earth and sky—
minerals arriving
to become heavy fruits mid-air—
you bend, and yet you hold,
host to all manner of birds
to welcome, each day, the dawn;

while the sea,
continually,
sings songs,
stories of ebb and flow,
miracles of rainbows
casting light
in myriad moments of Grace.

You speak,
without syllables,
and yet
hearts can hear
your voice
proclaiming,
"Resilience! Abundant Beneficence!

Life!"
Ya Hayy!
Ya Qadir! Ya Muqit!
Ya Razzaq!
Ya Wadud!

Roses of Your Love

Bismillah arRahman arRahim!
A new day—
Your Light reaches
the trees,
this heart.
Thank You
for the waters
of Your Grace
that wash clear,
again, this body
housing Your Name.
So many gifts
You have given,
and keep giving.
Roses of Your Love
inundate,
and I am well
in Your Seeing.
Alhamdulillahi, Ya Rabb al-'Alameen!
Ya Basir, Ya Wadud,
Ya Karim!

Don't You Love the Rain!

Don't you love the rain—
how it sounds, and swirls,
in puddles on the ground,
rippling in rings
with each drop?

How glorious
the warmth of summer,
after winter's demise,
dressed in early morning clothes
of deepest green,
rejoicing in renewal,
singing songs of remembrance
of absence,
and the coming harvest
engendered
by Your Everlasting Love.

Sparkles on the Sea

Your Words dance like sparkles on the Sea.
In any moment
we catch a glance,
a glimpse of Your
Eye
of Light,
calling to us, to dive
into Your Ocean,
that we might immerse in Your full resonance.
Buoyed by Your Love,
we float between sun and water,
open to Your Light,
and hearing
the silence of Your depths.
Your breeze carries us
through Your gently rippling waves,
a boat alive
with Your Love
and catching
fish of Your meaning
through every pore
that knows instinctively
how to open and close
to receive Your sustenance
and breathe out Your Name.
Ya Haqq, Ya Wadud,
O Truth, O Love!

Full Moon

The patterns of the moon—
why do we not pay attention?
If we were fishermen
we would be watching
the tides
and every glory
of Your evenings
and Your mornings,
the sky at sunset and sunrise.
"Red sky at morning—
sailors take warning;
red sky at night—
sailors delight."
The sky,
the breeze,
the moisture on the air
foretell the storms.
Native peoples know;
why have we forgotten?
Have we so distanced
ourselves
from Your elements
that we no longer re-member
of what we,
ourselves, are composed?
You write
upon the waters every day.

If we do not pay attention,
it will vanish,
and we will miss it—
the messages You would convey.
The waters of the mind,
where do they come to rest?
In the Harbor of Your Love,
in Your Welcoming Embrace.
Ya Wasi,
Ya Razzaq,
Ya Wadud!

At the Table of Your Grace

Huuu-ray!!
Today a Monarch
has come,
and in regal splendor
sips from the milkweed planted
in hopes of its arrival.
It drinks deeply
of Your nectar
from Your clusters,
then circles round
and lands
again
upon another,
fanning its wings
slowly
in Your sun.
How grateful this heart,
to see it—
another example of Your
Knowingness—what food
is right for whom,
and how we find it,
sense it out,
from Your Knowing in us,
through us, guiding us
to the best source of nourishment.

Still, it remains,
among the bees
who also dance
amid the rosiness,
choosing a blossom here
and there,
fluttering
among the grace-full
branches.
The bees, the butterfly,
they give each other space;
there is room for all of us
at the table of Your Grace.

Remembrances of Love

Bismillah arRahman arRahim.
Your Love encompassing—
dewdrops gather on the leaves
and fall to thirsty roots;
Your water finds its way
from sky to earth.
Bathing us with Your Breath
You awaken us to a new day.
We laugh in Your surrender
and weep when we forget—
that You are the Mover,
the Creator,
the One with whom we walk,
and rest,
all our days
and nights.
Owls keep calling
for hours—
Huuu is near!
And once again a glorious rain in the night—
and now,
once again, the day,
awash with Your Light!
Ya Karim! Ya Wadud! Ya Wadud!

Giving Birth

You expand us
to contract us,
to give birth,
and to breathe
in
Your
Grace.
Dawn has arrived,
and Your breeze surges,
rustling the crab apple leaves,
swinging the red fruits in Your sky.
With each breath
I offer this day to You,
but what do I have to offer
but You,
who have given everything,
and keep giving,
Eternally!
Ya Quddus,
Ya Samad!
O You, Most Holy and Pure,
O Eternally Self-Subsisting One!
You who satisfy all our needs
before we even recognize them,
as they emerge from the Sea
of Your prayer,
and we call out

Your Name,
as we sing to each other by heart,
and birth these miraculous
children of Love—
"And wherever you are, I am with you."

On the Street of Your Love

I need
to go out
for a walk
on the street of Your Love.

Birds fly,
but we have feet
to feel Your ground,

though we
have taken lessons
from their wings
and would also soar
in moments
of awakening.

2.
Miracles
abound in skies of Grace,
in ocean depths,
in mountains standing
firm in Your Love—
seen and Unseen—
ever You are near.
We come,
empty-handed,
and yet, You have gifted us
with so many skills.
Loving lingers with us,
as we return to Your door
through the dark side
of the moon,
until a new month
is born
and we arise again,
radiant.

Moment by Moment

Everything is alive with meaning.
The winter of water has passed.
A rock rose blooms in the garden;
at first sight, we know Your Love.

Moments of Grace

Western tanagers are here—
bright bursts of yellow
in the eucalyptus and podocarpus trees.
How do they know
the loquats have ripened?
They only ever come
during loquat season;
hue to hue they resonate,
and with nearby silk-oak blossoms.
Nectar abounds in plumbago
and bottlebrush
and lingering orange blossoms.
April blossoms into May,
and bird voices honey the air,
as roses rise in exaltation
and we know—
always, You are here.

Hasbiyallah!

Bismillah arRahman arRahim!
A new morning—
a day of Your Loving;
night has unfolded,
opened into Light.
These eyes,
of Your Grace and Giving,
perceive so many gifts—
endless to count!
Every breath a new knowing—
how could we ever
offer sufficient thanks?
You are the All-Sufficing.
To You we turn,
within You we rest
and find renewal
in Your Being—
Ya Awwal, Ya Akhir,
Ya Warith,
Ya Wadud!
You who Resurrect us
every moment,
Ya Ba'ith!
You who Respond to Prayer,
Ya Mujib—
You who are our prayer,
from the very beginning,

and now,
and ever after,
as we move,
and know this being,
as Yours.
Ya Haqq, Ya Wadud!
Ya Quddus! Ya Wadud!
Ya Zhul Jalali wal-Ikram!

Ulul Albab

A new day dawns,
fire in the heart,
and green hills
encourage
our fecundity—
roses and jasmine,
grains of the earth,
kernels of knowing
planted deep in our souls
burst forth
with songs of sustenance—
praises
for the One
who gives us birth!

Songs of Praise

The balance
of power
lies within
the *Fatiha*—
all praise is God's,
for there is
no one here
but He/She—
the One who is
creating,
not created,
who feeds us
when we forget
how
to feed
ourselves,
or what
our real food
is.
Breath
by breath
You unveil
our Essence,
turning us
from the darkness
into Light!

Living in the Miraculous

What do You say
to the trees
every spring
that makes them unfurl
their leaves,
each in a pattern
of family,
designed
in Hidden Realms?
Every year
we watch this miracle
and do not see.
We watch the flowers
burst through their buds,
sepal by sepal,
petals yearning
for the breeze,
to shake out their skirts
and dance awhile
within the warmth
of Your smiling sun,
and yet we do not see.
We watch Your birds
soar through Your air
to gather twigs
to build their nests
in crooks of trees

welcoming,
in window ledges,
beside our beds,
and, still, we do not see.
We watch the earth
burst with new green,
all sizes and shapes,
from within the darkness,
stretching tall
to catch your rain
and radiance,
channeling it,
down to thirsty roots,
and, still, we do not see.
We awaken every day
to miracles
of eyes and ears,
of taste and touch,
and fragrance—
how can we not know
how much You love us
and all of Creation?!
Ya Khaliq, Ya Bari, Ya Musawwir—
Ya Wadud!
Ya Karim!
Ya Razzaq!
Ya Quddus!
Holy Spirit
is re-birthed
from us
every breath
we breathe
in remembrance.
Subhanallah!

Ya Mu'id!
Ya Awwal!
Ya Ahkir!
Ya Haqq!

A Moment's Breath!

Bismillah arRahman arRahim,
You focus this heart
in realms beyond her knowing.

A moment's breath,
a new dawn—
Your gifts
are so immense!
How can we begin
to even acknowledge
all the ways
You care for us?
What can we give?—
"A heart torn open with longing."

From Darkness into Light!

O Allah!
Your dawn arrives
Illumined in the clouds—
the darkness intensifies the Light.
When our light diminishes,
You give us increase—
before, behind;
above, below;
to the left and to the right;
that we might see,
and know
the beauties
of our own hearts—
the garden You nourish
with Your Sun
and the Rain of Your Beneficence.
Grace abounds
amidst our challenges,
And surely,
with every difficulty
comes ease.

Gracious Rains

New mornings
awaken us;
summer rains have arrived
and Your top-most branches
bend
with the weight
of Your Grace.
Even a mountain
would fall to its feet
if You fully
revealed
Your Face.
In the Presence
of Your Power
the winds are scattered
and the clouds disperse.
Your Sun rises
in our hearts,
and all we know
is LOVE.

Subhanallah!

It is a new day.
The sun rises,
the light shines,
the trees are still green!
Surprises?
Are You not Amazing?!!
Words travel far,
from heart to heart;
streams of meaning
flow
into the Sea,
and we are renewed,
reborn,
as an aspiration
of Your Love.

"I so loved to be known
that I created the two worlds—
seen and Unseen—
so that My Treasure
of Generosity
and Loving-Kindness
might be known."

Subhanallah!
Ya Rabb al-'Alameen!

Exaltations of Your Love

Bismillah arRahman arRahim!
How gracious Your arrival,
every morning with the Light
and through the darkness
holding us in absence
of any-thing but You.
Night or Day,
You are with us,
this breath—Your Companion
for us, in us—
and these hearts
continually pulsing
with Your Love!
Hu, else, could be so Generous?!
Every particle
alive with Your Knowing!
Ya Wadud! Ya Karim,
Ya Haqq, Ya 'Azim!
Ya Zhul Jalali wal Ikram!
Subhanallah, Ya Rabb al-'Alameen!
Ya Nur, Ya Quddus,
Ya Allah!

Your Light Keeps Pouring!

Now,
Your light is pouring!
As the full glory unfurls,
our hearts rejoice
and swim in that Sea
that every morning
awakens us
to another Day of Grace.
So many gifts You give us,
our hearts weep
at Your attention.
How carefully You send us
everything we need.

Still, patiently, Your doves
wait upon the wire
for our neighbor
to fill the feeders,
and Your glorious hawk arrives
circling the cell tower,
until it lands in its uppermost branches
from where it has a vista
to find its food.

Communication happens
in invisible ways;
from here to there

my heart sends missives.
They fly upon Your air
across the ocean,
to find Your hearts
and nestle there,
to speak of love
and gratitude,
and whisper
of the Grace that finds us
every morning,
and every evening,
whenever we turn
to see Your Face,
and look into Your Eye
that shines so brightly
within our forehead,
beaming light through the darkness
to illuminate these bodies,
hearts, and souls—
breath
by breath.

Disappearing Within Your Love

Beloved,
so close You draw us,
inscribed in Your Heart.
The dogwood leaves
have turned red with longing
to return,
and the redbud hearts
flutter to earth
in their readiness;
everything is dancing its way
to You,
from You,
and within You.
Sometimes we forget to look
to see how much we are all held
within Your Beauty.
The breeze keeps whispering,
lifting all Your leaves
to flag our attention:
"I am here."
We breathe,
and know Your Name
within us,
written so long ago
upon these hearts
that appear
within Your Beauty

and disappear
within Your Love.
Ya Jamil, Ya Wadud,
Ya Haqq!
O You Who Are Beauty,
You Who Are Love!
O Truth!

Witness to Your Love

We are all witness to Your Love,
in every breath,
in every ripple of our flesh
as we walk about Your paths
among the palms
and dance in Your salty sea.

Your air breathes us, around us,
Your bougainvillea bursts into magenta bloom.
Your trees rain coconuts and purple cainitos;
oranges, coriander, and pineapple,
blended, refresh our nerve
to turn in ecstatic surrender,
to hear from every direction Your Word.

Voices and hearts share Your communication
among all these friends from different nations.
O You who understand all tongues,
help us to see
that we are all already knit together,
for all Eternity—
You are "we"; it is —
Your shawl, Your grass,
Your prayer, Your ocean,
Your hermit crabs, Your shifting sands,
Your sand-dollars and pelicans,

Your hummingbirds, Your raccoons,
Your ants, Your iguanas,
Your stars, Your moon, Your sun . . .

even if we disappear
below the watery horizon,
Your remembrance holds us within You,
for You are all that is,
All that ever was or would be,
the First, the Last,
the Living, the Loving,
Ya Wadud!
Subhanallah, Ya Rabb al-'Alameen!
Ya Allah HUUUUUUUUUU!!

The Garden of Your Exaltations

The Garden
of Your Exaltations
is forever pouring love
through the rivers
beneath these hills
of being.

From within the mountains
sparkling springs emerge
carrying fertility
to the valleys
embracing Your Growth—
trees to give us shade
and crops to feed
our hunger.

La ilaha il Allah—
only You,
only You,
every thing
is a mirror
where we can see
Your Truth.

Look deeper:
La ilaha il Allah.

No reality
but You.

Morning Opens

Morning opens,
again, to refresh
these nerves,
wired, conducted, into Your Beauty.
You smile,
through Your leaves,
Your flowers,
Your birds,
and this body
reverberates
with every strand
of cellular permission
to inhabit Grace.
Why are we here,
but to witness
in awe
all the inter-weavings
of Your Majesty and Glory?
To listen
to Your Song
through these ears—Your ears—
that channel
to the ocean
of our hearts—
these hearts
that can know
in a moment

the origin
of our sight,
the tenderness
with which we are welcomed
upon our return,
and the strength
with which we are held,
here, now,
with every breath,
recognized—
Subhanallah,
Ya Rabb al–'Alameen!
Glory be to You,
Sustainer of All Worlds!

Bees of Your Haven

Nothing would exist
without Your Love.
Bees find
their way
to sip
a flower's fragrance;
we find our way
to nestle
in
Your Sanctuary,
everywhere
abundant,
pouring sustenance,
through the keyhole
to Your refuge.
Light finds its way
through every crack
in our defenses;
the door,
You set,
we forget
to open,
flies wide
to welcome all souls
who turn
in recognition
of the Source

of all that nourishes,
all that heals
our riven bones,
our fractured hearts,
our complicated minds.
Untangled, restored,
in the shade of Your Love,
the sunshine of Your Grace,
we rest
upon the grass
soft as a willow's down,
along the river's side,
where the table is set,
and all
are invited,
always, and now.

Eternal Love

O *Allah!*
Ever You are Here,
and There,
and everywhere
these minds might traverse—
beyond all
our simple imaginings
of space or time—
sublimely Real,
stretching our cellular awareness
across realms
of knowingness.
Whose expanse are we?
Didn't You say,
"and spacious is My earth!"?
How can we
not know You know
us through You,
in our deepest heart,
where we are alone
with You?
Shedding our cocoons
of thought
and baggages of years,
we melt—

like a candle,

like water
returning
to its Source,
lifted
beyond the known worlds
to a placeless Place,
where we
are no longer "we"
but You,
in stillness
breathing,
being breathed;
All that ever has been,
is now,
or ever could be—
Ya Hafiz,
Ya Awwal, Ya Akhir,
Ya Warith!

Reflection Notes

1 (p. 1). *A Song in Praise of the Sacred:*
   from the ocean realms of Maui, Hawaii.

2 (p. 4). *A Breath of Love:*
   Ya Rabb al-'Alameen, O Sustainer of all Worlds!
   Ya Sami, Ya Basir, O You Who Are All-Hearing! O You Who Are All-Seeing!
   Ya Wasi! O You Who Are All-Encompassing!
   Ya Nur, Ya Wadud, O Light! O Love!

3 (p. 6). *Ah this Beauty:*
   love songs from Kauai, Hawaii.

4 (p. 8). *In the Palace of Your Love:*
   from the Hidden realms of Escondido, California.
   See *Surah al-Anfal* 8:12: *And always You are with us.*
   Ya Quddus, O Most Holy and Pure!
   Ya Wadud, O Infinitely Loving One!
   Ya Karim, O Infinitely Generous One!

5 (p. 9). *In the Name of All:*
   first published in *The Way of Mary, Maryam, Beloved of God,* p. 409.
   Salamun qawlan min Rabbin Rahim: See Qur'an, *Surah Ya Sin,* 36:58. *"Peace!" A Word from our Sustainer, Most Merciful.*
   Subhanallah! Ya Rabb al-'Alameen, Glory be to God! O Sustainer of All Worlds!
   Ya Khaliq, Ya Bari, Ya Mussawir, O Creator! O Patterner! O Bestower of Form!
   Ya Awwal, al-Akhir, Ya Warith, O You Who are the First, the Last! O Ultimate Inheritor of All That Is!

6 (p. 12). *A Mouth to Drink Your Love:*
   first published in *The Way of Mary, Maryam, Beloved of God,* p. 50.

7 (p. 13). *The State of Greenness:*
Putney, Vermont, on Dusty Ridge, just after the birth of our first granddaughter.

8 (p. 17). *"Am I not Your Lord?":*
see Qur'an, *Surah al-'Araf* 7:172.

10 (p. 20). *Freedom Celebrations:*
Love'ville, Kentucky, 4th of July.

11 (p. 21). *The Rain is Pouring Love:*
"See how God provides!" Qur'an, *Surah al-'Imran,* 3:37.

12 (p. 22). *Adab için:*
"For the purpose of Spiritual Courtesy," being re-membered, resonating in Love.

14 (p. 24). *In the Morning:*
See Hadith of Prophet Muhammad conveyed by Aisha:
It was narrated that 'Aishah said:
"I noticed the Messenger of Allah (peace and blessings be upon him) was missing [from bed] one night and I found him prostrating, with the tops of his feet facing toward the Qiblah. I heard him saying: *A'uzhu biridaka min sakhatika, wa a'uzhu bimu'afatika min 'uqubatika wa a'uzhu bika minka la uhsi thana'an 'alayka anta kama athnayta 'ala Nafsika.* (I seek refuge in Your good pleasure [with us] from Your stringency [that realigns us]; I seek refuge in Your clearing forgiveness from Your chastisement [that clarifies us]; I seek refuge in You, from You. I cannot praise You enough; You are as You praise Yourself)." The waters of Grace keep pouring!

15 (p. 25). *Your Joy is our joy!:*
"Love'ville," Kentucky, August on Cherokee Rd.
You are always with us. See Qur'an, *Surah al-Hadid* 57:4:
He is with you wherever you are.

16 (p. 28). *Planting Joy:*
   Ya Fatah, al-'Azim! O Opener, the Most Magnificent!
   Ya Wadud, al-'Alim! O Infinitely Loving One, the All-Knowing!
   Ya 'Aziz, al-Karim! O Almighty, Most Dear, the Most Generous!
   Subhanallah! Ya Rabb al-'Alameen. Glory be to God! O Sustainer of all Worlds!

17 (p. 30). *Exaltations:*
   "Love'ville," Kentucky, September.
   "the people who gather in remembrance": *Ahl azh-Zhikr.* Qur'an, *Surah an-Nahl,* "The Bee," 16:41–43.
   Ya Hu, O Holy Presence, *al-'Azim,* the Most Magnificent!

19 (p. 33). *The Day is Promised:*
   see Qur'an, *Surah al-Imran,* 3:8–9:
   "O our Sustainer, do not let our hearts swerve from the Truth, after You have guided us, and from Your Presence, gift us with compassion. Truly, You are the Giver of Gifts! [Rabbana, la tuzigh qulubana ba'da izh hadaytana wahab lana min ladunka rahmatan innaka anta al Wahhab.]
   "O our Sustainer, truly You will gather humankind together to witness the Day, about which there is no doubt. Truly God never fails to fulfill His/Her Promise."

20 (p. 35). *So Many Mornings:*
   "You love us, and we love You!" See *Surah al-Maidah 5:54, He loves them, and they love Him.*

21 (p. 37). *Bow in Worship!:*
   "Be still and know that I am God." See Bible, Psalm (of Prophet David) 46:10–11: "Be still and know that I am God. I will be exalted among the nations; I will be exalted in the earth. The Lord of all forces is with us!"
   And see, also, Psalm 62:5: "For God alone, O my soul, wait in silence, for my hope is from Him."
   Bow in worship and draw near. See Qur'an, *Surah al-'Alaq,* 96:19, of the first verses conveyed in the unfolding revelation of the Qur'an,

while Muhammad was in retreat in the Cave of Hira within *Jabal an-Nur* ("Mountain of Light").

This offering was first included in *Ramadan Love Songs*, p. 28.

22 (p. 38). *The Breath of Life:*
"Love'ville," Kentucky, Summer.

Ya Hayy, O Ever-Living Enlivening One! *Ya Qayyum,* O Eternally Self-Subsisting One, who root us in Your Being!

23 (p. 40). *The DNA of Joy:*
Ya Nur ala Nur ala Nur! O Light upon Light upon Light!

24 (p. 42). *Signs of Life:*
Ode to a Palm, Kauai, Hawaii.

Ya Hayy, O Ever-Living Enlivening One! *Ya Qadir,* O Infinitely Powerful Apportioner! *Ya Muqit,* O Nourisher (on all levels)! *Ya Razzaq,* O Provider (of everything)! *Ya Wadud,* O Infinitely Loving One!

25 (p. 44). *Roses of Your Love:*
Alhamdulillahi, Ya Rabb al-'Alameen! All praise belongs to God, O Sustainer of All Worlds! *Ya Basir,* O You who are All-Seeing! *Ya Wadud,* O Infinitely Loving One! *Ya Karim!* O Most Generous One!

28 (p. 47). *Full Moon:*
back porch, "Love'ville," Kentucky, late summer.

Ya Wasi, O You Who Encompass us, embracing us always, *Ya Razzaq,* O You Who Are Continually Providing for us, in profound and subtle ways, *Ya Wadud,* O Most Loving One!

31 (p. 52). *Giving Birth:*
"Love-ville," Kentucky, Autumn.

Ya Quddus, O Most Holy and Pure! *Ya Samad,* O Eternal Satisfier of All Needs (who Yourself are without need)!

"And wherever you are, I am with you." *Witness your Sustainer inspired the angels to convey His Message to the faithful, "I am with you."* [Qur'an, Surah al-Anfal 8:12]

35 (p. 58). *Hasbiyallah!:*
"Divine Reality is Sufficient!"

Ya Awwal, O You who are the First! *Ya Akhir,* O You who are the Last! *Ya Warith,* O Inheritor of All! *Ya Wadud,* O Infinitely Loving One!

Ya Ba'ith, You who Resurrect us every moment! *Ya Mujib,* You who Respond to Prayer!

Ya Haqq, Ya Wadud! (O Truth! O Love!), *Ya Quddus! Ya Wadud!* (O Most Holy and Pure! O Love!), *Ya Zhul Jalali wal-Ikram* (O Lord of Power and Magnificent Generosity!)

36 (p. 60). *Ulul Albab:*
"People of the Kernel," "People of Insight." See Qur'an 3:190: *Truly in the creation of the heavens and the earth and the flowing interchange of night and day are Signs for Ulul Albab.*

~ Escondido ("The Hidden Realm"), 2024.

37 (p. 61). *Songs of Praise:*
See Qur'an 1:1: *All praise is God's, Sustainer of All Worlds!*

38 (p. 62). *Living in the Miraculous:*
Ya Khaliq, Ya Bari, Ya Musawwir—Ya Wadud! Ya Karim! Ya Razzaq! Ya Quddus! O Creator! O Patterner! O Bestower of Form!—O Infinitely Loving One! O Most Generous One! O Provider of All! O Most Holy and Pure!

Subhanallah! Ya Mu'id! Ya Awwal! Ya Ahkir! Ya Haqq! Glory be to God! O Restorer! O You who Are the First! O You Who Are the Last! O Truth!

39 (p. 65). *A Moment's Breath!:*
"A heart torn open with longing." *Mathnawi* of Jalaluddin Rumi, Book I:3.

40 (p. 66). *From Darkness into Light!:*
And surely, with every difficulty comes ease. Qur'an, *Surah al-Inshirah* 94:5–6.

41 (p. 67). *Gracious Rains:*
Even a mountain
would fall to its feet
if You fully
revealed
Your Face.
See Qur'an, *Surah al-A'raf* 7:143:
As soon as his Sustainer revealed His Glory to the mountain, it crumbled into dust, and Moses fell down unconscious. So when he awakened, he said, "Limitless are You in Your Glory! [Subhanaka!]

42 (p. 68). *Subhanallah!:*
"I so loved to be known
that I created the two worlds—
seen and Unseen—
so that My Treasure
of Generosity
and Loving-Kindness
might be known."
~ Hadith Qudsi—saying of the Divine beyond the Qur'an—conveyed through the heart of Prophet Muhammad, peace and blessings be upon him.
Subhanallah! Ya Rabb al-'Alameen! Glory be to God! O Sustainer of All Worlds!

43 (p. 69). *Exaltations of Your Love:*
Ya Wadud! Ya Karim, Ya Haqq, Ya 'Azim! Ya Zhul Jalali wal Ikram! Subhanallah, Ya Rabb al-'Alameen! Ya Nur, Ya Quddus, Ya Allah! O Infinitely Loving One! O Most Generous One! O Truth! O Most Magnificent! O Lord of Power and Magnificent Generosity! Glory be to God! O Sustainer of all Worlds! O Light, O Most Holy and Pure! O Divine Reality!

44 (p. 70). *Your Light Keeps Pouring!*
See Qur'an, *Surah al-Baqarah* 2:115 : *Wherever you turn, there is the Face of God.*
and Qur'an, *Surah an-Nur* 24:35:

God is the Light of the heavens and the earth.
The parable of His light is,
as it were, that of a niche containing a lamp;
the lamp is enclosed in glass, the glass like a radiant star;
lit from a blessed tree—an olive-tree
that is neither of the east nor of the west—
the oil of which would almost give light
even though fire had not touched it: light upon light!
God guides to His light the one who wills to be guided;
and God offers parables to human beings,
since God has full knowledge of all things.

45 (p. 72). *Disappearing Within Your Love:*
"Love'ville," Kentucky, Autumn.

46 (p. 74). *Witness to Your Love:*
offered in Costa del Oro, Costa Rica.
Ya Wadud!
Subhanallah, Ya Rabb al-'Alameen!
Ya Allah HUUUUUUUUUUU!!
O You Who are Infinitely Loving!
Glory be to You, O Sustainer of All the Worlds!
O Divine Reality, Infinite Presence!

49 (p. 80). *Bees of Your Haven:*
See Qur'an, *Surah an-Nahl*, "The Bee," 16: 68–69:
And your Sustainer taught the bee to build its cells
in hills, on trees, and in dwelling places,
then to eat of all that the earth produces
and to skillfully find the spacious paths of its Lord.
There issues from within their bodies a drink of varied hues
containing healing for human beings:
truly, in this is a sign for those who reflect.
See Bible, 23rd Psalm of Prophet David: 1–6:
The Lord is my shepherd; I shall not want.
He makes me lie down in green pastures:
He leads me beside tranquil waters.

He restores my soul:
He guides me along the paths of righteousness
for His name's sake.
Even though I walk through the darkest valley,
I will fear no harm: for You are with me;
Your rod and Your staff, they comfort me.
You prepare a table before me
in the presence of those who challenge me:
You anoint my head with oil; my cup overflows.
Surely goodness and love will follow me
all the days of my life:
and I will dwell in the house of the Lord forever.

See Qur'an, *Surah Maryam* 19:60–62:
For the faithful who do the deeds of wholeness and reconciliation will enter the Garden, Gardens of Eternity (beneath which rivers flow) . . . and they will hear there greetings of Peace. And there they will receive their sustenance, morning and evening.

See also Qur'an, *Surah Az-Zukhruf* 43:70–73:
Enter the Garden, you and your spouses, rejoicing.
To them will be passed around dishes and goblets of gold;
there will be there all that their souls could desire,
all that could delight their eyes; and you shall abide there.
Such will be the Garden of which you are made heirs
for your deeds of wholeness.
There you shall have abundant fruit,
from which you shall have contentment.

See also Qur'an, *Surah Ar-Rahman* 55:76–78:
Reclining upon meadows green and rich carpets of beauty—
which, then, of the favors of your Lord will you deny?
Blessed be the Name of your Lord,
the Lord of Power and Abundant Beneficence!

50 (p. 82). *Eternal Love:*

Qur'an, *Surah al-Ankabut* 29:56. "*and spacious is My earth!*"

Ya Hafiz, Ya Awwal, Ya Akhir, Ya Warith! O Protector and Preserver, O You Who are the First, O You Who are the Last, O Inheritor of All That Is!

Other Publications by Camille

(sweetladypress.com; sufism.org)

The Way of Mary: Maryam, Beloved of God

Ninety-Nine Names of the Beloved, Intimations of the Beauty and Power of the Divine

Words from the East
Poetic reflections, first in the series of "Songs of the Soul"

Ramadan Love Songs
Poetic reflections, second in the series of "Songs of the Soul"

The Light of Dawn, Daily Readings from the Holy Qur'an

Women of Sufism, A Hidden Treasure: Writings and Stories of Mystic Poets, Scholars, and Saints
(which brought to light the integral contribution of women to the spiritual path of Islam)

Rumi's Sun, The Teachings of Shams of Tabriz
Excerpts from the *Maqalat* of Shams-i Tabriz translated by Refik Algan and Camille Helminski

Rumi and His Friends, Stories of the Lovers of God, Excerpts from the Manaqib al-'Arifin of Aflaki
Selected and translated by Camille Adams Helminski with Susan Blaylock

The Qur'an, Volume I through XI:
   The Qur'an Volume I: Surahs 1–3
   The Qur'an Volume V: Surahs 16–19
   The Qur'an Volume XI: Surahs 67–114
   The Qur'an Volume VI: Surahs 20–23 (Forthcoming January, 2026 Inshallah)

TRANSLATIONS with Kabir Helminski:

The Rumi Daybook, 365 Poems and Teachings from the Beloved Sufi Master
Selected and translated by Kabir Helminski and Camille Helminski

Jewels of Remembrance, A Daybook of Spiritual Guidance from the Wisdom of Mevlana Jalaluddin Rumi
Selected and translated by Kabir and Camille Helminski

Rumi Daylight, A Daybook of Spiritual Guidance: Three Hundred and Sixty-Five Selections from the Mathnawi of Mevlana Jalaluddin Rumi
Translated by Camille and Kabir Helminski

The Pocket Rumi (Shambhala Pocket Classics)
Edited by Kabir Helminski (translations by Kabir and Camille)

Happiness without Death, Desert Hymns
Assad Ali, translated by Camille Adams Helminski, Kabir Helminski, and Dr. Ibrahim Al-Shihabi

Civilization of Paradise, Revelation Poems
Asad Ali, translated by Kabir Helminski with Camille Helminski, Mahmoud Mostafa, and Ibrahim Shihabi

ANTHOLOGIES for THE BOOK FOUNDATION

The Book of Nature, A Sourcebook of Spiritual Perspectives on Nature and the Environment
The Book Foundation Education Project Series, edited by Camille Helminski

The Book of Character, An Anthology of Writings on Virtue from Islamic and Other Sources
The Book Foundation Education Project Series, edited by Camille Helminski

OTHER COLLABORATIVE TRANSLATIONS

Awakened Dreams, Raji's Journeys with the Mirror Dede
Ahmet Hilmi, translated by Refik Algan and Camille Helminski

The Mevlevi Wird, The Prayers Recited Daily by Mevlevi Dervishes (the tradition of Rumi)

Mevlevi Adab and Customs
Abdülbâki Gölpınarlı, translated by Refik Algan and Camille and Kabir Helminski

RECORDINGS:

Glorious Morning Light (Quranic recitations by Camille)

The Mevlevi Wird

Rumi's Sun, Excerpts from the Teachings of Shams of Tabriz

You Are Joy (Rumi recitations by Kabir and Camille with Sufi music from around the world)

Garden within the Flames (*ilahis* sung by Kabir and Camille—Dost Quartet)

www.ingramcontent.com/pod-product-compliance
Lightning Source LLC
Chambersburg PA
CBHW031425290426
44110CB00011B/529